MW01223183

Introducing

Clarinet
Trios

Easy trios for beginners

James Rae

www.**universal e dition**.com
vienna · london · new york

UE 21 311
ISMN M-008-07651-0
UPC 8-03452-02408-8
ISBN 3-7024-2875-5

To the teacher

In his own teaching, James Rae places significant emphasis on music making with others encouraging the pupil to listen and to 'carry on' whilst at the same time focusing on her or his own part. To this end he has written a number of duets, trios and quartets. His *Eyes and Ears* sight-reading series and well-known tutor *Introducing the Clarinet* embrace this concept with duet parts included for the teacher lending support and encouragement.

Complementing the tutor, *Introducing Clarinet Trios* includes pieces that are all in the low register. The parts are of the same technical level and are written, with practical tips along the way, to familiarize players with a new set of considerations, to become a good team player and above all to experience the enjoyment and satisfaction of making music with others.

These trios can be used in group teaching, on the concert platform and in examinations. *Introducing Clarinet Duets* and *Introducing Clarinet Quartets* are also available.

To the pupil

Ensemble music, that is to say music for two or more players, can be described in basic terms as either:

homophonic where all parts *generally* follow the same rhythm as, for example, in the well-known Christmas carol *Silent Night* or the anthem *God Save the Queen*, or,

polyphonic where all parts *generally* move independently in counterpoint, as in a fugue or a canon, eg *Frère Jacques*. The word literally means 'many sounds' and is perhaps already familiar to you in connection with advanced mobile phone ring tones which are made up of more than one musical line.

I use the word 'generally' as many ensemble pieces contain both of these compositional devices.

In the first section of the book we will deal with strictly homophonic pieces as I feel that this is the most secure way of introducing the concept of playing together. The second section will deal with polyphonic pieces and in the third section we will combine both of these elements.

James Rae, February 2005

Liebe Lehrerin, lieber Lehrer!

In seinem eigenen Unterricht legt James Rae großen Wert auf gemeinsames Musizieren, wodurch die Schüler nicht nur lernen, sich auf ihre eigene Stimme zu konzentrieren, sondern auch zuzuhören und „durchzuhalten". Zu diesem Zweck komponierte er eine Anzahl von Duetten, Trios und Quartetten. Schon in seiner Serie *Eyes and Ears* (Übungen zum Blattlesen) und in seinem bekannten Lehrbuch *Introducing the Clarinet* äußerte sich diese Überzeugung in den zur Unterstützung der Lehrer und zur Ermunterung der Schüler beigefügten Duettstimmen.

Als Ergänzung des genannten Lehrbuchs gibt es nun *Introducing Clarinet Duets*. Hier bewegen sich alle Stücke in der tiefen Lage. Alle Stimmen haben den gleichen Schwierigkeitsgrad und enthalten praktische Hinweise. Die Spieler sehen sich in diesen Stücken mit neuen Problemstellungen konfrontiert und entwickeln dabei einen Teamgeist. Vor allem aber sollen hier der Spaß und das Vergnügen am gemeinsamen Musizieren vermittelt werden.

Diese Trios können im Gruppenunterricht, im Konzertsaal und bei Prüfungen herangezogen werden. Darüber hinaus sind auch die Bände *Introducing Clarinet Duets* und *Introducing Clarinet Quartets* erschienen.

Liebe Schülerin, lieber Schüler!

Ensemblemusik, also Musik für zwei oder mehr Spieler, kann grundsätzlich in zwei Arten unterteilt werden:

Homophone Musik, in der alle Stimmen *prinzipiell* dem gleichen Rhythmus folgen wie zum Beispiel in dem bekannten Weihnachtlied *Stille Nacht* oder in der britischen Nationalhymne *God Save the Queen*.

Polyphone Musik, in der sich alle Stimmen *prinzipiell* im Kontrapunkt wie in einer Fuge oder einem Kanon (z. B. *Bruder Jakob*) unabhängig voneinander bewegen. Das Wort „polyphon" heißt wörtlich übersetzt „viele Klänge" und ist dir vielleicht schon durch Handy-Klingeltöne vertraut, die aus mehr als einer musikalischen Linie bestehen.

Ich benutze das Wort „prinzipiell", weil viele Ensemblestücke beide Kompositionstechniken enthalten.

Im ersten Abschnitt dieses Buches findest du homophone Stücke, weil ich glaube, dass man dadurch das Konzept des Zusammenspiels am sichersten erlernen kann. Der zweite Abschnitt enthält polyphone Stücke, und im dritten Abschnitt kombinieren wir die beiden Elemente.

J. R.

Cher professeur!

Dans ses propres cours, James Rae accorde beaucoup d'importance à la musique d'ensemble : ses élèves doivent apprendre à s'écouter et à « faire avancer le morceau » tout en se concentrant sur leur propre partie. Dans ce but, il a composé plusieurs duos, trios et quatuors. Par exemple, sa série *Eyes and Ears,* consacrée à la pratique du déchiffrage, et la célèbre méthode *Introducing the Clarinet* comprennent des duos qui permettent au professeur d'encourager l'élève en jouant avec lui.

Introducing Clarinet Trios complète la méthode en proposant des pièces toutes écrites dans le registre grave. Les deux parties sont du même niveau technique. Assortis de conseils pratiques, ces duos aideront les clarinettistes à se familiariser avec une situation nouvelle, à acquérir l'esprit d'ensemble et surtout, à découvrir le plaisir et la satisfaction de jouer à plusieurs.

Ces trios peuvent être utilisés pour des cours collectifs, des auditions ou des examens. Il existe également un recueil de duos et un de quatuors (*Introducing Clarinet Duets* et *Introducing Clarinet Quartets*).

Cher élève!

La musique d'ensemble, c'est-à-dire à deux musiciens ou plus, peut être décrite schématiquement comme :

homophonique lorsque toutes les voix suivent *en général* le même rythme, comme dans un cantique, par exemple le cantique de Noël *Douce nuit* ou le *God Save the Queen.*

polyphonique lorsque les voix suivent *en général* un rythme différent, en contrepoint, comme dans une fugue ou un canon, par exemple *Frère Jacques.* Le mot « polyphonique » signifie littéralement « plusieurs sons », et vous l'avez peut-être déjà rencontré à propos des téléphones portables, pour décrire les sonneries composées de plusieurs lignes mélodiques.

Je précise « en général » car dans la plupart des pièces pour ensemble, on rencontre les deux procédés de composition.

Dans la première partie du recueil, vous ne trouverez que des pièces strictement homophoniques : je pense en effet que c'est la manière la plus sûre de s'initier à la musique d'ensemble. Les pièces de la deuxième partie sont polyphoniques, et dans celles de la troisième, ces deux éléments sont associés.

J. R.

Homophonic Trios

1. Introit

Top tip: Always listen out for who has the upper part. It is not neccessarily the first player!
Folge immer der Melodiestimme. Die hat nicht immer Spieler 1!
Essayez toujours d'entendre qui a la mélodie. Ce n'est pas toujours la première clarinette !

2

2. Ceremonial Fanfare

Top tip: Always be on your toes when counting in 3/4. The first beat of the next bar comes sooner than you think!

Sei immer auf der Hut, wenn du im 3/4-tel Takt spielst. Die erste Zählzeit des nächsten Takts kommt früher als du denkst!

Restez vigilants quand vous êtes en 3/4. Le premier temps de la mesure suivante arrive plus vite qu'on ne le pense !

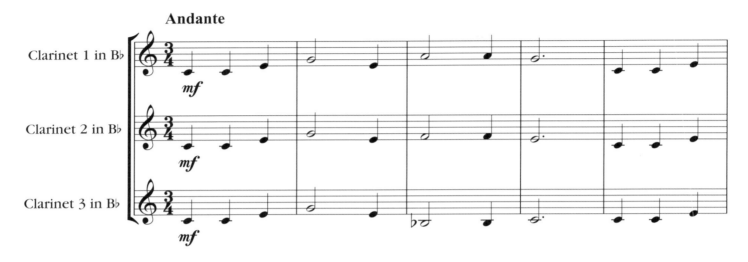

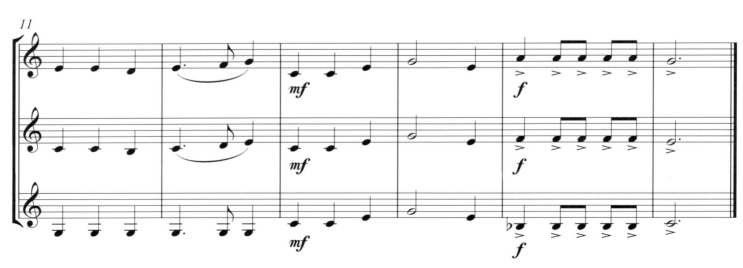

3. The Chase

Top tip: Aim to match all the quavers to achieve a secure sense of ensemble.
Versuche alle Achtelnoten gemeinsam mit den Mitspielern zu spielen,
damit ein Gefühl sicheren Ensemblespiels entsteht.
Jouez bien les croches ensemble, le morceau doit donner une impression de stabilité.

4. Smith's Cove

Top tip: Observe all articulation markings and make them match between all three parts.
Beachte alle Artikulationszeichen, und stimme den Klang mit den anderen beiden Stimmen ab.
Respectez toutes les articulations, vous devez jouer tous les trois les mêmes.

Polyphonic Trios

5. Ancient Hymn

Top tip: Aim to bring out the moving part and keep the longer accompanying notes in the background.
Remember, the main melody can appear in any part. Always be aware of this.
*Versuche, die sich bewegende Stimme hervorzuheben und die längeren begleitenden Noten
im Hintergrund zu halten. Denke immer daran, dass die Hauptmelodie in jeder Stimme auftauchen kann.*
Faites ressortir la mélodie et ne jouez pas trop fort les notes longues qui l'accompagnent.
Souvenez-vous : ce n'est pas toujours la première voix qui a l'air principal. Pensez-y !

UE 21 311

6

6. The Legend

Top tip: Always give the notes their full value to allow the chords to resonate clearly.
Halte die Noten immer ihrem vollen Notenwert entsprechend aus, damit die Akkorde voll klingen können.
Jouez toujours les notes jusqu'au bout pour qu'on entende clairement les accords.

7. Fairground Waltz

Top tip: Count your rests very carefully!
Zähle die Pausen äußerst sorgfältig!
Comptez très soigneusement vos silences !

UE 21311

8

8. Spinning Jenny

Top tip: Aim to keep the quaver movement continuous so that there are no detectable breaks in the line.
Versuche die Achtelbewegung so gleichmäßig wie möglich zu spielen, damit keine hörbaren Brüche in der Linie entstehen.
Soutenez les croches pour qu'on n'entende pas de rupture dans la ligne mélodique.

Concert Pieces

These pieces combine homophonic and polyphonic writing.
Diese Stücke kombinieren homophone und polyphone Musik.
Ces pièces associent l'écriture homophonique et polyphonique.

9. Windsor Walkabout

Top tip: Don't forget that this piece has two minim beats per bar. Crotchets are only worth half a beat.
Vergiss nicht, dass man in diesem Stück die halben Noten als Grundschlag zählt.
Viertelnoten gelten deshalb nur als eine halbe Zählzeit.
N'oubliez pas que la mesure est à deux blanches. Les noires ne valent que la moitié d'un temps.

10. Deep Pan Boogie

Top tip: Keep this in a solid 4 and count the rests very carefully in part 3.
Zähle hier gleichmäßig den 4/4-Takt und beachte in Stimme 3 sehr sorgfältig die Pausen.
Gardez bien un rythme à 4 et comptez très soigneusement les silences dans la 3ᵉ partie.

11. Celtic Lullaby

Top tip: This piece is a good exercise in intonation as it is based on perfect 4ths.
Listen very carefully to each other as you play.
Dieses Stück ist eine gute Intonationsübung, da es auf reinen Quarten beruht.
Höre beim Spielen sehr genau auf die anderen Spieler.
Cette pièce en quartes justes est un bon exercice pour travailler l'accord.
Écoutez-vous très attentivement.

12. Branch Line Toccata

12

Top tip: Don't forget that we are in 2/2. Crotchets = 1/2 beat, minims = 1 beat and semibreves = 2 beats.
Vergiss nicht, dass dies ein 2/2-Takt ist. Viertel = 1/2 Schlag, halbe Note = 1 Schlag und ganze Note = 2 Schläge.
N'oubliez pas que nous sommes en 2/2. Les noires valent 1/2 temps, les blanches 1 temps et les rondes 2 temps.

UE 21 311